BRING YOUR LIFE BACK TO LIFE

A GUIDE TO EFFORTLESS JOY

BRIAN ANDREAS

A HUNDRED WAYS NORTH

ISBN 978-0-9981490-0-4
LCCN 2016915579
Copyright ©2016 by Kai Andreas Skye

Because here's the thing: Fia & I are the two people behind A Hundred
Ways North. It's a place where we discover every day how people can
make a life together. What we discover ends up in our books & our
workshops & in our conversations with everybody we meet. Obviously,
there's a lot to say about this whole process. (Which is one of the reasons I wrote this book.) Here's how to contact us:

A HUNDRED WAYS NORTH
PO Box 131,
Decorah, IA 52101
USA

Brian: brian@ahundredwaysnorth.com
Fia: fia@ahundredwaysnorth.com
www.ahundredwaysnorth.com

First Edition: *November 01, 2016*

To my beautiful Fia Skye. Every day I'm grateful for all that you bring to this life of ours. For the stories you bring home from Rigby. For the compass you carry in your heart that somehow points North & West at the same time. Most of all, for your clarity & willingness to be all of you with all of me. I am honored to be your mate...

To my readers, especially you who've held my words close to your heart for a very long time. You already know that my writing is a way I listen to the divine. But our conversations on facebook & instagram & in real life, have taught me that it's also a way the divine speaks to you. Thank you for opening your hearts to me so these words land safely. It is a gift I continue to treasure...

Other books by Brian Andreas:

Mostly True
Still Mostly True
Going Somewhere Soon
Strange Dreams
Hearing Voices
Story People
Trusting Soul
Traveling Light
Some Kind of Ride
Peculiar Times (e-book)
Theories of Everything
Something Like Magic
Impossible to Know

With Fia Skye:
Creative Anarchy

With Lorne Resnick:
Cuba: This Moment Exactly So

BRING YOUR LIFE BACK TO LIFE

A GUIDE TO EFFORTLESS JOY

BOX OF
OLD RULES
THaT'S AL-
MOST
COMPLETELY
FULL
BECAUSE
We don't
Have a
Lot of TIME
for Stuff
that Doesn't
WORK
any More

A week ago, just as I was finishing this book, I had a dream. In it, I was in a room with three women. One of them, my first love, took both of my hands & looked in my eyes & told me I could do better. The other two made sounds like the murmuring of morning doves. I asked how I could do better. She said, tell the truth. I looked at the other two. They both nodded. Yes, tell the truth, they said.

I listened. The truth is Bring Your Life Back to Life is a book I've been living for the past few years. Writing it all down was an obvious next step.

Looking back, it's easy to see it was always right there in front of me. Simple. Clear. Seeing it only required a few things. Like giving up my ideas of how life should go. Letting go of the separateness I fought so long to keep & simply allowing myself to be how I am in every moment.

The biggest thing it required, though, was asking myself how long I wanted to pretend that I'm in this life alone...

Turns out the answer is I don't want to pretend that any more, ever again. Because it's simply not true.

Quite a few years ago, I had a conversation in Berkeley with a poet I knew. He had quite the reputation in academic circles. His work was dense & unmistakably Poetry-To-Be-Reckoned-With. That day, I was just sitting there quietly, watching my sons dig in the dirt for treasures that only very small boys can find, when he walked up. He mentioned that he'd just finished a new book of poetry & would I like to hear one of his favorites? It was one of those perfect fall days, with the wind & the smell of fallen leaves wrapped up in sunlight. I thought Why not?

The most astonishing thing happened. He spoke, with a voice resonant with love & longing & a sense of the bigness of all things & the words he spoke were so simple. Five or six lines. That was all.

I knew his other poetry. This was nothing like that. This was a poem that went directly to the heart of things, without apology. It's beautiful, I said. Yeah, he said. It's not my usual crap. Cancer'll do that to you. He looked over at the boys playing. His eyes glistened. I want my grandson to know who I am someday, he added. So, I don't have time to lie any more.

A lot has changed over the past few years. For me. For all of us. It feels to me like we're in a very big moment, coming back to who we really are. Coming back to the truth that all of us are in this world together. We don't have time to lie any more. It may feel hard along the way, but I've experienced that coming out the other side into the joy of being fully alive together is worth it. So. Worth. It.

So, I offer this, a simple guide to effortless joy. No excess. No unnecessary explanation. Simply a guide that was useful to me along the way. I hope you find it useful, too. Because I'd like nothing more than for you to have your own joy fully in this world with us all...

With love,

Brian Andreas
Decorah, Iowa
September 17, 2016

There actually aren't any
secrets to life.
It's all right there
in front of you
all the time.

Mainly, it just depends
on what you're ready
to hear.

Do not wait to be
who you want to be.
Start today.

If the universe disagrees,
it'll let you know.
But usually it only disagrees
when you're trying
to be someone else.

You learn how to do life
by doing it.

You learn more slowly
if you think you're
one of the people
who can skip this part.

You know
exactly what to do next
& when you think you don't,
it's usually because what's
next
is cleaning up something
you knew not to do
in the first place.

If this is not
the life you want to live,
stop.
Go in another direction.
Do this
as many times as it takes
to live that life.

Don't be surprised
if it takes barely any time at all
when you start to do this...

The life you have
is actually all you need
to get the life you want.

& everything
in this life you have
is there
to help you see that.

When you think
you're missing something,
you usually aren't.
You're most likely
looking so closely
at all the things you expect
to be there
that you don't see
the other things
that've been there
all along.

There's not much
you can't do
if you simply ignore
what you think
is possible
& just get out there
& live
with your whole
wild heart.

You'll make mistakes.
Try not to make them
more than once.

Though, to be fair,
each mistake
is always
a little bit different.

If you're not making mistakes,
it means
you're probably living
someone else's idea
of life.

Which is actually
one of the bigger mistakes
you can make.

There is no such thing
as a perfect version of you.
Every day, you'll make
choices that change
who you're going to be.

Who you're becoming
is not finished.
Which means you can
be different,
no matter who you've been
up until now.

Nothing
is teaching you
a lesson.
Or teaching someone else
a lesson.

There's only this:
who do you want to be?
&
are you being that?

When you finally
let people
love you
exactly the way they do,
it's pretty easy to see
that's all
they've ever been
trying to do
the whole time.

You have never been
in this exact moment before,
so you don't have to pretend
like you know
exactly what to do.

Just so you know,
it's going to be like that
your whole life.
That's what makes it all
so interesting.

You can spend a lot of time
trying to do things
for the right reasons,
when mainly,
if you just do things & see
how they work out,
you can pick a reason afterwards
that makes it sounds like you knew
what you were doing
the whole time.

The funny thing is that
doing things this way,
it's likely you'll find
your own right reasons.

#1. Say yes
   to things that bring you joy.

#2. Say no
   to things that don't

#3. If you're tempted
   to say maybe,
   say no.

It's all
in how you choose,
unless you choose
wrong.

Then, it's all
in how you laugh
about it
together.

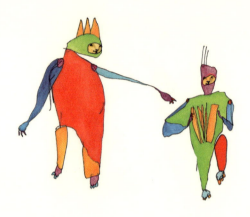

Making plans
for your life
doesn't get you out of
the stuff that comes along
whenever it feels like it.

The stuff that comes along
whenever it feels like it
might actually be
what gets you to your life
faster.

At some point,
you'll probably hear
someone say
there's only love & fear.
The truth is
there's really only Love.

Sometimes,
it takes being afraid awhile
to see that.

One day,
you just choose to be certain.
Which is not the same thing
as knowing everything.

It's more like this:
what you know
is exactly what
you need to know
to start. Whatever it is.
The rest is learning
as you go.

People act like certainty is an illusion. It's not.
It's a choice & it changes your whole life.

Live
without waiting to see
if it turns out all right.

Because,
honestly,
your idea of right
is a lot smaller than
right
actually is.

There is no right way
to do
life.

There's only
stuff that works
& stuff that doesn't.

& you're the one
who gets to decide.

A lot of people will tell you
that you have no control
over how you feel.
This is not true.

You can feel however you'd like,
any time you'd like.

Go ahead & try it.
Imagine something
that gives you joy.
Got it? Now, go
& be like that
all day long.

Yes. It is that simple...

There are times
you'll get stuck
because you want to know
the right answer.
The problem is
you already know.

You just don't like
what the answer is telling you
you'll have to give up.

Which is usually
a different answer.

It's pretty easy
to have a simple life
once you give up
trying to explain
everything you do
to yourself
&
everybody else
you know.

Everything
is right here.
If you can't see it,
it's because
you can't see it.
Not because
it's not here.

Remembering
how to see better
is the whole point.

It's ok
to let go
of stuff you learned
a long time ago,
especially
when you figure out
it's completely wrong.

There'll come a moment
when you see how you've bent
yourself into a shape
that fits the people you've known
& you see
how that has to stop
& though it's not always easy,
that's exactly where you begin
to find out
who you're meant to be.

You will look back
more often than you think
& wonder if you could've
done it differently,
forgetting always
that the you who thinks that
needed to do
that first thing
first.

THIS is the thing He's been chasing after His whole life & now that he's close enough to see what's in it, He's thinking of chasing after something else

If you never do the thing
that really, truly
lights you up,
you'll die a little inside
every day
until, after awhile,
you find you're mainly
just waiting for it
to end.

Life
is actually easier
when you're not checking
all the time
to see
if everyone else agrees
it's a life
worth having.

You can just decide
to be happy & not
have to explain it
all the time
to people who decided
you shouldn't.

Doubt
is mainly just you
thinking
someone else
might not agree
that this is how
you go about having
a perfectly fine
life.

If you never ever think
for your whole life
about
who you are,
or who you're going to be
someday,
you'd still end up being it,
except
you'd be less anxious about it
along the way.

It's pretty easy
to have a life you love
once you decide
to have it
right now
instead of waiting
until after
you get all the other things
you think you need
first.

When you quit
defending the stuff
you think you know,
there's a lot more room
to simply be there fully
with all the things
you don't.

Which is pretty much all of it.

Absolutely
everything you do
is a chance
to give
love.

Start
any time
you'd like.

It's generally a good practice
to say yes to life,
since even if you say no,
life is going to go ahead
& do it anyway.

You may have
very good reasons
why something
is not possible,
but
don't be surprised
if someone else
goes ahead & does it
anyway,
because they have
very good reasons
why it is.

You believing
that you're right
doesn't mean
someone else
is wrong.
It just means
that you've stopped
being curious
about what you don't know
now.

You are the home you need
& sometimes
you won't see that
until the day
you leave the places
you aren't at home,
but stayed
all those years
anyway.

There's magic
everywhere
all the time
& when you're
having a hard time
seeing it,
it's usually because
you've already decided that
if it was really magic,
it'd look like something
else.

It doesn't take much
to begin to remember
your own life.
Only understanding
that every bit of it
is moments
you've
never
had
before.

One of the fastest ways
to stop being confused
is to ask your body
what's going on & then
actually listen,
instead of
immediately thinking,
Oh, it's probably
something else.

Life
changes
when you understand
all the way
to the heart of you
that there's only you & me
catching each other
when we fall
& standing up again
& seeing
if we can do it better
this time.

Every moment
you sit around
trying to predict
the exact best thing
to do next
in your life
is a moment you miss
being in it
& letting life tell you
what comes next.

If you just want to be happy
most of the time,
you can skip everything else
& just do this:

#1. Don't spend a lot of time
explaining to other people
what makes you happy.
Just go ahead
& do it.

#2. Stay away
from people who are unhappy
most of the time.

The thing that scares you
most
is usually the key
to who you really want to be.
Once you quit hiding
from the thing that scares you
most.

When you're ready
to speak truth,
don't expect
someone else
to go along
with it.

Because
they usually won't.

Especially if they're
on the other side
of the untrue thing.

You're exactly
what the world
needs,
in case you're wondering
if it's time
to get started.

& even if you're not,
what's the point of waiting
when you could be
out living?

It's much easier
to quit worrying
about what
other people
think of you
when you remember
you're going to die,
no matter what.

After that,
you can worry about it
for as long as you want.

Be clear on this:
you will die
some day.

Until then, though,
this is the life you have
& why
would you waste
a minute of it
loving
with anything less than
your whole self?

Life is always giving you
the exact answers
to your questions,
often
before you even think to ask.
So if you're getting tired
of the same answers
all the time,
maybe it's time to ask
different questions.

It's so simple
you may not see it
for a very long time,
but it takes your whole life
exactly how it is
to understand
that all you are
is the one
who gets to love.

Just because
you can wrap your words
around something
& have it make sense
(more or less)
doesn't mean
there's any good reason
to believe it.

Listening to the voice in your head
is only a good idea if
all the other parts of you
already agree.

You get to listen
to anyone you want,
but if
they keep telling you
to be afraid,
you might
want to get
a second opinion.

The simplest way
to happiness
is to let yourself be
happy
with the things
that make you happy.

Also, stop wondering
about whether
you could be happier
with other things
you don't know about yet.

If there's no joy in it,
whatever it is,
it's because there's no love,
no matter how many people
tell you it's just
how things work
around here.

Doing things the way
everyone else does them
only works if
you discovered it
for yourself
& it just happens
to look like the way
everyone else does it.

More often than you think,
you'll find yourself
having to choose
between safety & adventure.
Trust your own wild heart
to choose
the best way.

But just so you know,
the best way
is not always
safe.

You'll pick
an idea of how to live
& then off you'll go
until you figure out
you don't need an idea,
that you can just live
without anything more
than loving
every moment,
the best thing is try
to pick an idea that
doesn't break your spirit
when you get it
wrong.

Who you are
is not
who you think you are.
You are much, much bigger.
The only reason
you pick smaller
is because
you're used to it.

The unexpected thing is that
when you decide to be bigger,
you'll see how much bigger
everyone else is, too.

It's your life.
You can be
exactly as big
as you want.
You don't even need a reason.
So, if you pick
a size that's not right,
all you have to do
is say Oh well
& go
& pick another one.

At first,
a lot of this will seem
unbelievable.
But then, bit by bit,
you start to notice
when it happens.
That's a good time to know this:
you don't have to believe
any of it's possible.
It happens all the time
whether you believe it or not.
You just might want to
quit working so hard
to ignore it
when it does.

A very short checklist. Refer to as needed.

#1. If it's in your life,
　　 you might as well play with it.

#2. If it's no fun to play with,
　　 why
　　 is it in your life?

Ask questions
that really matter to you
if you want to have
a life that really matters
to you.

If you'd rather
have a life with
no surprises,
ask questions
you already know
the answers to.

It's a strange thing
to understand that
you only have questions
because you stopped listening
to the answers
in the first place.

A more or less complete
practice of living:

Listen quietly
when you don't know
& wait
to act
until you do.

Notice how easy it is
to come up with reasons
why this won't work
in your particular situation.
Mainly because
it's hard to admit
you prefer acting
over listening.

It's enough
to pay attention to
the little things.
The steam rising off
that first cup of coffee.
Sunlight
coming through the window.

There's no right answer
for what's going to make you happy.
There are only these little things
that add up to how you spend your days.
It can take you a long time
to see a life
is actually nothing
more than that.

All I can tell you
is there will come a moment
when you see how easy it is
to have the thing you want
& all that stopped you
the whole time
was believing
it had to be harder.

This world
is amazing
& you'll forget that
again & again
your whole life.

But if you
remember
more than you forget,
you'll be fine.

A note from Brian

Not long ago, a young woman came up to me after a public talk in North Carolina. I love your words, she said. They take all the chaos & make it clear. It wasn't until later on that I thought that it's only chaotic in the first place because our idea of life is smaller than life itself. Which is why lately I'm tending towards having fewer ideas about anything. Especially life.

Also, I have a feeling that life feels perfectly fine as it is & doesn't think of itself as chaotic at all...

Most of these started as secrets. As in these-are-secrets-to-living-I-noticed-along-the-way. That seemed like a perfect place to start a book until the day I was writing & these words showed up: there actually aren't any secrets to life. It's all right there in front of you all the time. Mainly, it just depends on what you're ready to hear.

Fia says this is almost the book I meant to write. That it's more like a handy guide to have nearby for quick reference when something baffling shows up along the way. Because let's be clear. None of these words are a substitute for your own knowing. You'll always know better than someone else who's looking out of a completely different life. But, sometimes, having a place to start is all you need. A place to say Oh yeah, that's in the general direction of what I'm seeing. Or, Oh no, that's not it at all. We find our way by taking a step along the way we're finding.

As for it being almost the book I meant to write, I have to agree. But it's a step along the way I'm finding. I look forward to hearing your experience of it. Feel free to leave me a note on Instagram (@brianandreas), or drop in at A Hundred Ways North to find out where we are in person, either at one of our Creative Anarchy workshops, or at one of our community conversations around the country.